# A Walk with God for Teens

# A Walk with God for Teens

## for Teens

Brief Meditations and Prayers for Teenagers

## Jason Moore

**DIMENSIONS**
FOR LIVING
NASHVILLE

A WALK WITH GOD FOR TEENS

*Copyright © 2005 by Dimensions for Living*

*This book is printed on recycled, acid-free, elemental-chlorine–free paper.*

**Library of Congress Cataloging-in-Publication Data**

ISBN 0-687-05412-5

Library of Congress Control Number: 2005925225

05 06 07 08 09 10 11 12 13 14 — 10 9 8 7 6 5 4 3 2 1

MANUFACTURED IN THE UNITED STATES OF AMERICA

# It's Like Butter

*Surely you desire truth in the inner parts;*
*you teach me wisdom in the inmost place.* —**Psalm 51:6**

—w—

Do you know how hard it is to find real butter? Not long ago, having decided to cook something that required more than opening a can and turning on the stove, I was easing through the grocery store, recipe in hand, looking for butter. I had no idea there were so many kinds of fake butter. But I didn't want those. I wanted real butter.

Honestly, I doubt if it would have made any difference in the recipe. One was probably as good as another. There are times in life, however, when an imitation just won't do. I should know. For most of my life I had an artificial, imitation faith. I went to church, and I knew all the right things to say, but that didn't make it real.

That's the way it is with butter. On the outside, it all looks the same. You can't tell the real from the fake just by looking at it. Yet one look at the ingredients, and you'll see the difference. The same is true for us. It's what is inside that counts. God sees through our pretending; he knows if we truly love him or if we're just putting on a show.

**Lord, I confess that sometimes my faith is just a show. In these coming days, increase my faith and my commitment to you. Amen.**

# Starting with Myself

*"Why do you see the speck in your neighbor's eye, but do not notice the log in your own eye?"* —Matthew 7:3 NRSV

———∿∿∿———

I can't leave well enough alone. If I have an itch, I'll scratch it until it creates a sore. Then I'll scratch that 'til it bleeds. *Then* I'll keep at it until it leaves a scar. Of course, I know better. I should take Mom's advice: "Stop picking at it; leave it alone." That's easier said than done. See, I'm a perfectionist, and that itch, bump, or sore represents an imperfection. So I keep fiddling with it, trying to make it better. Most of the time, however, it just gets worse. A little red dot becomes a big, painful dot, which is not what I intended at all.

Sometimes we do the same thing to people. We see an imperfection in someone in our life, and we think, *Hey, I bet I can fix that.* So we "scratch" and suggest and insinuate until we've made that person sore, unhappy inside, or unhappy with us. But why this urge to fix others? Why not start with ourselves?

Our tendency is to find fault in others. After all, this is usually easier than owning up to our own mistakes. Yet before we can be a guide for others, we must take an honest look at ourselves. Until we can see our own shortcomings, we can't really help anyone else.

**Lord, show me the areas in my life that need work. And when it comes to an "itch," help me know when to leave well enough alone. Amen.**

# The Wrong Places

*How can young people keep their way pure?*
*By guarding it according to your word.* **—Psalm 119:9 NRSV**

---

As I was standing on the lip of a large, green dumpster, it occurred to me that this was not the best way to spend the afternoon. But there I was in my khaki pants and button-down shirt, nosing through the trash, looking for a phone number I'd misplaced. The search did not go well: by the time I'd gone through the last bag of trash, I was out of places to look and just about out of patience.

After washing up, I flopped into my chair and wondered how I could lose that number. It seems I'm constantly misplacing important papers and throwing away what I should keep. Then, on a hunch, I began flipping through my Bible. Sure enough, there was the missing number, jammed way back in the concordance.

Why is the Bible often the last place we look? Not so much for misplaced numbers, but for answers. Why are we more accepting of the morals and views of our favorite sitcom than those prescribed by God? Maybe it's because Jesus' call to holiness and service seems too hard. It's just easier following the ways of the world. But the easy way isn't always the best way. If we want to be more like Jesus, we need to study his Word. After all, we can't expect to find the right answers by looking in the wrong places.

**Lord, help me live according to your word. Amen.**

# Good Fences

*The LORD commanded us to obey all these decrees and to fear the LORD our God, so that we might always prosper and be kept alive, as is the case today.* —Deuteronomy 6:24

———

Out here in the field the grass is tall and green; the fence that surrounds it is high. It's a good place for my dog, Jake, to stretch his legs, to do the running he can't do in the house. It's good for me, too. I like to see him run, with his ears flying back and his tail wagging as he gallops along. From where I sit, the field looks big, vast, like a prairie. But Jake doesn't care for fences. He doesn't understand there's danger waiting for him on the other side. He just wants out.

Jake spends most of his time making laps around the field, trying to find a place where he can squeeze through or dig out. Out in the open, I call him. I've got his rope bone; I'm ready to play. But Jake is still doing laps, still looking for a way out, imagining that what's on the other side of the fence must be better.

Sometimes I find myself doing the same thing. I think of all that God requires, and it's hard not to feel fenced in. Yet I know God's laws are good fences. They are for our safety and well-being. God knows what's on the other side, and the danger of digging out.

**Lord, help me to enjoy life within the boundaries you've created. Amen.**

# Digging Out

*I waited patiently for the LORD;*
*he turned to me and heard my cry.*
*He lifted me out of the slimy pit.* **—Psalm 40:1-2**

—ɯ—

It seemed like a good idea at the time. That's all I can say in defense. After all, my Jeep wasn't designed to be a bulldozer. Too bad that fact didn't occur to me until after I'd sunk it to the frame. No, all I had thought about was that big pile of gravel in the driveway. It looked like it would take a few hours to spread by hand. So instead, I had decided to use my Jeep: Just drive over it a few times and save all that shoveling for another day. Well, it almost worked. *Almost.*

It was dark when I finally got her out. By then the sun had disappeared and had taken with it my pride. I was ashamed of my laziness and impatience. Worst of all, I was beginning to see a pattern. How many times had I grown impatient with God, tried to rush things, only to make a mess.

I am thankful, however, that God never abandons us. Even when we are at our lowest, he doesn't leave us wallowing in the mud. Cry out to God and he will lift you up; he will give you a firm place to stand.

**Lord, thank you for sticking by me when I mess up. Amen.**

# Ironing It Out

*You see, at just the right time, when we were still powerless, Christ died for the ungodly.* —**Romans 5:6**

Every now and then, a strange craving comes over me. I get the most incredible urge to—*iron*. Now, I know what you're thinking, especially the guys: this isn't the manliest of urges. Maybe if I wrestled a grizzly bear, then that would be something to write home about.

But that's not what I do. Instead I just grab a shirt or a pair of khakis, heat up the iron, and go at it. The iron feels good in my hands, and I like watching the wrinkles disappear. You don't have to use much pressure, but I like to press down hard, to feel like I'm the one smoothing out those mountains of khaki and cotton.

If only it were that easy in my spiritual life. An iron, some starch, and *presto!* I could just steam all the doubt and disappointment, all the sin and uncertainty away. Too bad it doesn't work that way. See, we're limited; we don't have the power or the perspective to do it right. It's like trying to iron a shirt with you still in it. It just won't work. It's only when we give the "iron" to God that all our sins are smoothed away.

**Lord, smooth out the wrinkles of my sin. Amen.**

# Leaving It Behind

*As far as the east is from the west,*
  *so far has he removed our transgressions from us.* —**Psalm 103:12**

—⟡—

A car parked behind my apartment hasn't moved for weeks. I think it's been abandoned. I pass it every morning when I walk my dog, Jake: a little white car with Michigan tags, full of stuff it looks like they didn't want anymore. It's like they got tired of all that junk and decided they were better off without it.

It makes me wonder, *wouldn't it be nice if I could get rid of all my junk?* Not the stuff in my closets or those old issues of *Sports Illustrated* I haven't thrown away, but rather the gunk that's collected in my soul: all those "boxes" stacked high with past mistakes, broken promises, secret sins. Wouldn't it be great if I could just drive it off somewhere and leave it behind?

Thanks to God, we don't have to drive anywhere. We just take it to him in confession. For whenever we truly repent, we are cleansed of all the mess clogging our souls. Somewhere beyond the horizon, they disappear into the infinite love and grace of God.

**Lord, thank you for taking away my sins. Amen.**

# Cleaning Out the Fridge

*Get rid of all bitterness, rage and anger.... Be kind and compassion-
ate to one another, forgiving each other, just as in Christ God forgave
you.* —Ephesians 4:31-32

—◦◦◦—

It was long overdue. I should have cleaned out the refrigerator
weeks ago, but I kept putting it off. I didn't want to see what was
inside. Let's see, there was the month-old milk, the brown let-
tuce, a black banana, and a box of aging pizza that looked like a
bad science experiment.

I know this sounds gross. But I bet we could all stand to clean out
the "fridge." Not the big, tall appliance in your kitchen, but our
hearts. Many of us have all this stuff stored up inside that we
don't need. There's a crisper full of past wrongs, and an egg crate
filled with hurts and insults, not to mention a carton or two of
spoiled dreams.

We can pretend it's not there, but it won't solve the problem.
Instead, a spiritual rot develops that steals the smile from our
faces and the joy from our hearts. But there is a solution. It's
called *forgiveness,* and it's better than industrial-strength cleaning fluid. It's God's way of cleaning out the gunk inside; in turn,
we must learn to forgive others just as God has forgiven us.

**Lord, help me let go of past hurts and disappointments.
Amen.**

# Lift Ticket

*The LORD himself goes before you and will be with you; he will never leave you nor forsake you.* —**Deuteronomy 31:8**

—∿∿—

The mountain was steep, and I was glad I didn't have to hike up it. Instead, I was breezing over it, floating on the ski lift, just biding my time until I reached the top. Up there, the air was cool and crisp, the snow pristine. Looking out across the mountains dressed so beautifully in white, it was hard to imagine a life more perfect or serene.

Beneath my dangling skis, however, the snow had begun to melt, revealing an odd assortment of bottles and containers among the rocks. There the snow was dirty, and I could see tracks where others had gone to retrieve their poles before making the long hike back up.

But that's how life is in a world muddied by sin: no one rides on the lift. We don't get carried over our problems; rather, we're down in the dirty snow, looking for our poles, struggling to make it up the mountain. Moreover, God doesn't beam us up at the first sign of trouble. Instead, he does something much better: he walks with us the whole way.

**Lord, thank you for always being with me. Amen.**

# Mixed Fruit

*Be joyful always; pray continually; give thanks in all circumstances, for this is God's will for you in Christ Jesus.* —1 Thessalonians 5:16-18

It was midafternoon and I was hungry, so I wandered down the hall to the kitchen to see if I couldn't scrounge up something to eat. Some days the results aren't good: one look inside the fridge, and I head straight to Chick-fil-A. But this was a good day, for there I found a bowl of mixed fruit.

Well, I sat right down and started munching. First I took care of the watermelon because it's my favorite. Then I ate the cantaloupe. I left the grapes for last. Some of these were getting a little squishy, so I had to pick around the bad ones.

Isn't it a shame that we can't do that in life? After all, wouldn't it be great if we could just pick around the bad days? I know I would. But life's not like a bowl of fruit. We can't pick our way through, enjoying the good days while altogether avoiding the bad. Rather, I think life is more like grape juice: all the grapes are crushed together, and we drink it. Sometimes we find the taste bitter, and sometimes we find it sweet. And though we did not choose the grapes that would be crushed into our cup, we can choose to make the most of every day.

**Lord, help me see life as a blessing. Amen.**

# Learning to Be Content

*I am not saying this because I am in need, for I have learned to be content whatever the circumstances.* —**Philippians 4:11**

———ᗰ———

After a long day of hiking, I pitched my tent and rolled out my sleeping bag for a well-deserved nap. I woke a few hours later, draped in the freshly fallen darkness, cold and hungry. *Nothing like a hot bowl of soup to warm your bones,* I thought to myself, *especially when you're on the trail.* So I got out my camp stove, turned the fuel valve, and lit a match. A beautiful blue-red flame leapt around the burner.

Just as quickly, however, the flame disappeared. I lit another match. Then another. And another. Same result. It just wouldn't stay lit. *Looks like no soup for me,* I pouted, as I ripped into yet another granola bar. My dog, Jake, was undeterred, however. My misfortune was his good luck, and he was quick to clean the soup can.

A few hours passed, and I couldn't sleep. Not because I was cold or hungry but because I was marveling at how picky I had become. I'd had my heart set on a warm meal, and I was disappointed that I didn't get what I wanted. In the process, I overlooked a great many blessings. All my needs were met: I had a warm place to sleep, food enough to eat, and even my favorite companion to warm my feet. There in that tiny tent, I was learning to be content.

**Lord, help me remember my blessings and be content. Amen.**

# Choosing Joy

*In this you greatly rejoice, though now for a little while you may have had to suffer grief in all kinds of trials.* —1 Peter 1:6

—∿—

I have no idea how it got up there, much less how it survived. After all, the ledge is too narrow to hold much soil and the brick too strong for tender roots to penetrate. Everything seems to be working against it, and yet, there it is, healthy and green, looking better than most of the plants in my house.

This has got me wondering about circumstances and survival, and why some people make it and other people don't; why some people flourish while others barely get by. Maybe it has more to do with your soul than the soil in which you're planted.

Through our relationship with God, we learn that joy is not based on external circumstances but on an inner condition of the spirit. We begin to understand that true happiness is found in loving and being loved by God. This is what enables us to see beyond our circumstances, to catch a glimpse of the eternal, to flourish no matter the condition of the soil.

**Lord, help me find joy in you. Amen.**

# Listening

*After the earthquake came a fire, but the LORD was not in the fire. And after the fire came a gentle whisper.* —1 Kings 19:12

———

Some time ago, I was having dinner with a friend at this neat little Chinese restaurant. We hadn't seen each other for a while, so we were busy catching up. Then it happened—a phone started ringing. Immediately, all conversation stopped as folks scrambled for their phones: women were digging through their purses, while men were fumbling through their jackets. Everything stopped because no one wanted to miss that call.

These days, many of us have a phone with its own personalized ring, and we know right away whether a call is for us or someone else. When our phone rings, the response is the same: we drop what we're doing right away, afraid to miss a call. Everyone wants to be connected and available.

Doesn't it seem strange how we make ourselves available to everyone but God? God is always there for us, ready to listen, but how can we make ourselves more available to him? The answer is simple but not easy: we must listen for his voice. Though God has never spoken to me from a fiery cloud (or called me on the phone), that doesn't mean he's stopped speaking. He still speaks through his Word. He still speaks through his creation. In fact, he speaks in a thousand different ways and often in unexpected places, if we are willing to listen.

**Lord, help me listen for your voice. Amen.**

# Baby Food

*In fact, though by this time you ought to be teachers, you need some-*
*one to teach you the elementary truths of God's word all over again.*
*You need milk, not solid food!* **—Hebrews 5:12**

—⁂—

Across the table sat my sister. She was holding Megan, my
niece, on her lap and flying a spoonful of applesauce toward her
tiny, scrunched-up face. Megan watched the spoon as it circled
closer and closer. Her hands waved wildly as she wiggled in self-
defense. Her mouth fell open just as the spoon swooped by; she
then frowned when she tasted the cargo.

It's been a few months since that day with the low-flying spoon
and an unhappy niece who didn't care for the cuisine. Megan's
almost a year old now. Soon she'll be rid of all that baby food,
and she will be able to do some serious eating. No more applesauce or pureed carrots for her, especially when she learns to
feed herself.

Sadly, some of us never seem to master this, at least when it
comes to spiritual food. We depend completely on others to feed
us instead of accepting responsibility for our own spiritual nour-
ishment. However, we are not babies who need to be spoon-fed.
We are capable of feeding ourselves by studying God's Word.
God appoints ministers and teachers to guide us, not to do the
work for us.

**Lord, give me a hunger for your Word. Amen.**

# Fireflies

*When I consider your heavens,*
*the work of your fingers,*
*the moon and the stars,*
*which you have set in place,*
*what is man that you are mindful of him,*
*the son of man that you care for him?* **—Psalm 8:3-4**

It's a short distance, but in the dark it seems farther. We walk cautiously beneath the oaks and poplars, across the other campsites to the grassy field. The field sits low and flat, pulled taut between the mountains. The grass glistens with dew. Somewhere in the dark, a stream is polishing stones, making our voices seem strange and out of place. We grow still. One by one, the flashlights click off and their circles disappear.

I've brought the campers here to see fireflies—to watch them flash and flame, to see them blinking like Christmas lights. I am waiting for them, scanning the dark. I wonder where they are. The others, however, have already forgotten them. They are standing with heads thrown back, their gaze fixed on the sky, amazed by the number of stars, amazed when one breaks loose and flames across the night. I miss out on this grand sight; I'm still looking for fireflies.

I wonder what else I've missed, how many blessings I've overlooked simply by focusing on the wrong things—brief flashes of light that promise great things but so seldom deliver. And yet, all the while, God's love and mercy shine like the stars.

**Lord, help me see the big picture and not be captivated by things that don't matter. Amen.**

# Holy Ground

*"Take off your sandals, for the place where you are standing is holy ground."* —**Exodus 3:5**

———

This wasn't how I envisioned my Labor Day weekend. I was supposed to be up in the mountains, away from the heat and humidity and headaches of life. But my parents' project took longer than expected. Saturday morning came, and I hadn't even begun working on the roof. I could forget about relaxing by a mountain stream. I knew how I'd be spending my weekend: sweating on the roof, laying shingles in the sun.

*So much for rest and relaxation*, I thought. So much for communing with God and watching the sun come up over the mountains. The only communion would be between my hammer and an apron full of roofing tacks. This certainly wasn't the spiritual retreat I'd hoped for.

Or was it? What did I lack? I was alone with my thoughts, alone on the roof. Why couldn't this be a sacred place? After all, God spoke to Moses while he was working, tending the flock—not at church, not on some spiritual retreat, but in the middle of an ordinary day. You see, God doesn't confine himself to Sundays or holidays or those rare times when we actually get a break. God can speak to us in, at, and through our work. With God, any place can be holy ground.

**Lord, help me see you in my daily routine. Amen.**

# Murphy's Oil

*Create in me a pure heart, O God,*
  *and renew a steadfast spirit within me.* **—Psalm 51:10**

—⁓⁓—

It's amazing what a bucket of warm water and a bottle of Murphy Oil Soap will do, especially to the old hardwood floors in my house. Say good-bye to dirt and grime. Adios to dog hair too. If only the floors would stay that way: shiny and clean and lemon-scented. If only. But that's not how it is. Jake is shedding as we speak. And I don't help matters much, either. It's not that I intend to make a mess. It's just the wear and tear of daily traffic, going in and out and in again, tracking in a little dirt each time. I sometimes wonder if the house is ever really clean at all, or if the effort of occasional cleaning is even worth it.

Come to think of it, I often wonder the same thing about life. It is very hard to have everything squared away all the time. I get behind. The laundry piles up. And the floors . . . well, let's just say that they could use some work. It's the maintenance that's hard.

The same is true for our relationship with God. It's not hard to get cleaned up just for Sunday. But what about the other days of the week? Are we spending time with God each day or are we putting it off for "some other time"?

**Lord, forgive me when I don't spend time with you each day. Teach me your importance. Amen.**

# Rattle and Hum

*"Be still, and know that I am God."* —**Psalm 46:10**

—∿—

A few years ago, someone decided that the radio in my Jeep would look better in theirs, so I awoke one morning to find a hole in the dash and an odd assortment of wires where my radio used to be. Thus began a period of unusually quiet drives to school, which, to be honest, I wasn't thrilled about.

Now I don't know about you, but my Jeep has a choir of rattles. Normally, I'd just turn up the volume and drown out the noise. All that changed, however, when my radio was stolen. There was no quick fix, no button to push to make it go away. Instead I found myself actually listening to the assortment of various rattles, pondering over the possible causes and cures, worrying over the potential costs.

We all have our own "rattles." Yet because we are so busy and distracted, we hardly ever turn the volume down and listen to what's going on inside. We like the noise; it's silence we find unbearable. If we could just learn to be still, to turn the volume down, we could better hear the voice of God speaking to our fears, hurts, and deepest longings.

**Lord, free me from the things that distract me from hearing your voice. Amen.**

# Learning from Others

*The clever see danger and hide;*
   *but the simple go on, and suffer for it.* —**Proverbs 22:3 NRSV**

—⚒—

The trail was slippery and steep. Often a fallen tree would block the trail, so we'd have to climb over or go around. Sometimes a crystal stream would meander through. Then we'd scramble across a makeshift bridge or leap from stone to slippery stone. Still, it wasn't particularly hard if you were careful.

For once, being last in line had its benefits. Every slippery stone and exposed root was discovered well before I reached it. Those in front slipped, tripped, or twisted first. Cries of "Watch out for that limb!" and "That rock sure is slippery!" made me more alert, and I altered my steps accordingly. The trouble spots were easy to recognize because of those who'd gone before me. By watching them, I was able to keep from falling.

We don't have to learn the hard way. We can learn what to do and what *not* to do simply by observing others. As a philosopher once said, "From the errors of others, a wise man corrects his own."

**Lord, help me learn from the mistakes of others. Amen.**

# Seeking God

*You will seek me and find me when you seek me with all your heart.*
*—Jeremiah 29:13*

———⟨⟨⟨———

Some people go to the beach looking for God. Others gaze at the water contemplating the mysteries of life. I go looking for shark's teeth. Walking slowly through the tide pools, I scan all the shell fragments for those tiny, black triangles. The water ripples in, churning the sand, clouding the water, and tumbling the shells before rolling out again. As the water clears, one suddenly appears. I pinch it between my fingers, rinsing it in the surf.

I used to think it was luck—being in the right place at the right time when the waves coughed one up in plain view. Now I know better. Luck has nothing to do with it; it's diligence. If you look long enough, eventually you will find what you are looking for.

It's that *long enough* part, however, that gives us trouble, especially when it comes to knowing God. We don't seem to have the time or the interest. If God doesn't show up immediately, we just move on to something else. Surely God wants us to know him, but that kind of knowledge won't come overnight or merely by warming a pew on Sunday. If we want a deep knowledge of God, we must study his Word and spend time with him in prayer.

**Lord, help me seek you as earnestly as you seek me. Amen.**

# Specially Made

*I praise you because I am fearfully and wonderfully made.* —Psalm 139:14

—⁓—

At fourteen, I was the shortest guy in the ninth grade. Even worse, almost all the girls were taller than me, and, I thought, *Who wants to go to the freshman dance with Mr. Short-stuff?* Of course, Mom and Dad tried to make me feel better. Mom bought me a new shirt, while Dad reminded me that he didn't really start growing until he was sixteen. But sixteen seemed light-years away, and though the new shirt was nice, it didn't make me look any taller. Any way you cut it, I was just plain short.

I'm twenty-seven now. I'm a little taller, though I'm not what anyone would call tall. If anything, I'm just average. No Hollywood good looks or NBA height, nothing to make you notice me in a crowd. In fact, by most people's standards, I'm extraordinarily ordinary. How about you? Does your appearance/height/weight set you apart or help you blend in?

Learning to be content with how God made us is hard, especially when TV and magazines practically scream that we have to look a certain way: tall and beautiful. Often, we look in the mirror and find it hard to get excited about what we see. But God loves how we look. He took great care in making us just the way we are. And if it's OK with the creator of the universe, it's all right by me.

**Lord, thank you for making me the way I am. Help me see myself as you see me. Amen.**

# Tearing Down

*Reckless words pierce like a sword,*
*but the tongue of the wise brings healing.* —**Proverbs 12:18**

—᙭᙭—

Give me a handful of teenagers and a few hours, and I can tear down just about anything. Just last Monday we were working on a house that needed a new roof. Before we could put on the new shingles, however, we had to tear off the old tin. Piece of cake; by ten o'clock in the morning we had the whole roof torn off. It took less than three hours.

Fixing it was another story. It took three days just to replace the front. We had to replace the rotten boards and cover it with felt, all before we could lay the first shingle. In the process, half of our roofing crew wandered off to find easier work.

Then again, it's always harder to build than it is to destroy. This is especially true when it comes to words. Maybe that's why we find it easier to say something harsh to someone rather than something kind. Maybe that's also why we spend more time gossiping and cursing than we do praising and blessing. It's just easier to tear down. *Easier* doesn't mean *better*, however. As Christians, we should strive to do the right thing, to say the kind thing, even when it is more difficult.

**Lord, help me use words to build up rather than tear down. Amen.**

# Perspective

*"In this world you will have trouble. But take heart! I have overcome the world."* —**John 16:33**

———✦———

When the van blew a tire on a deserted stretch of Interstate 64, with the wind whipping and the temperature just above freezing, I decided that God must be punishing me. Nothing had gone right since we pulled out of the church parking lot. Between the traffic and the road construction and the dinner that took *forever,* we were well behind schedule and well on our way to strangling each other. Now this. It couldn't have come at a worse time.

We climbed out of the van, hands plunged deep into our pockets, and surveyed the damage. It didn't look good: the right front tire was shredded. Well, staring at it wouldn't do any good, so we got out the jack and the spare and went to work. Forty-five minutes later, the spare was on and we were rolling. Two hours after that, we were warming ourselves by the fire in the hotel lobby, laughing about our trip.

It wasn't so bad. All the headaches and delays were inconveniences, but not true problems. It was just a matter of perspective. So often we let the little inconveniences of life throw us for a loop. We get all worked up when things don't go as smoothly as we'd like. But life is like that. It can be a lot of trouble. It often is difficult. But that doesn't take away from its beauty any more than thorns subtract from the beauty of a rose.

**Lord, help me keep a positive attitude when things don't go as planned. Amen.**

# The Harvest

*Then he said to his disciples, "The harvest is plentiful but the workers are few." —Matthew 9:37*

⎯⏋⎯

The fields are white with cotton. I noticed them the other day as I was driving home, rolling down a thin gray ribbon of road between the brown stalks and the slow, dying sun. And it got me thinking—the way a long car ride will at the end of the day, at the end of a week, at the end of a month that just seems to slip by unnoticed.

It's November already. I've been so busy I hardly noticed. But I noticed those white blossoms, those fields of strange flowers catching fire at dusk. Even at sixty miles an hour, I noticed. And I wondered to myself, *Who will pick it? Someone should be in the fields. Someone should be on a tractor. And yet the fields are empty. Will all this go to waste?*

Maybe Jesus was thinking the same thing as he looked out on the people who followed him from town to town to hear his teachings. They were hungry for the Word, eager for the kingdom. Today it's no different; people are still searching for meaning, only now we are the ones called to work in the fields. As believers, we know what matters most, and we can offer this truth to others—if we are willing.

**Lord, give me the courage to share your truth with others. Amen.**

# Lighten Up

*"Come to me, all you who are weary and burdened, and I will give you rest.... For my yoke is easy and my burden is light."* —**Matthew 11:28, 30**

—⚍⚍—

The first time I went backpacking I got everything wrong. Not only did I pack too much, I also packed the wrong things. I simply didn't need two pairs of jeans, three books, and four cans of soup for an overnight trip. Of course, you don't realize this when you're carrying your pack out to the car. After all, it's not *that* heavy, and you figure that having a little extra might come in handy.

Until you start hiking. Then it's a different story. Soon your back is hurting, your legs are aching, and the spectacular views you read about—well, they're not quite what you imagined. In fact, the only thing that is spectacular is how bad your feet hurt!

Since then, I've learned a lot about what to bring and what to leave behind—in backpacking and in life. Generally speaking, it pays to pack light. Instead of trying to please everyone else, try to please God. Don't worry about being the most popular, but be true to your friends. Learn to be content with what you have, and don't stress over having the latest gadget or keeping up with everyone else. You just might amaze yourself and your friends by how happy you are simply by packing light and packing right.

**Lord, help me hold on to what matters and get rid of what doesn't. Amen.**

# Rocking the Boat

*"For I am going to do something in your days
that you would not believe,
even if you were told." —Habakkuk 1:5*

———∿∿∿———

Not far from here, the Edisto River runs black and slow through the cypress trees. It's a good place to kayak, and there's enough current so that you don't have to paddle any more than you'd like. It seemed like the perfect place to spend a lazy Saturday with my dog, Jake. The trouble is Jake is not very fond of water. However, since he wouldn't actually be in the water, I thought he would be fine.

Looking back, *fine* was an overestimation. *Terrified* was more like it. And though this particular kayak was rated for fast-moving water, it was not rated for one large, frightened dog. So Jake stood and shook, and the kayak rocked and almost rolled. Now, I didn't have a problem with getting wet. I was prepared for a swim. Still, if I was going to take a dip, I wanted it to be on my own terms: with the kayak pulled ashore, and my dry clothes and lunch safely stowed away.

Sometimes we are like that when it comes to God. We want to meet God on our own terms, *when* and *how* it suits us. We really don't want anything out of the ordinary to happen that might make us uncomfortable. Yet often that's exactly what it takes for God to get our attention.

**Lord, shake me from my complacency. Amen.**

# An Endless Supply

*What then? Shall we sin because we are not under law but under grace? By no means!* —**Romans 6:15**

—⚶—

I'm not sure why they thought we needed so much toilet paper. After all, only four of us were sharing a bathroom in the dorm my freshmen year. Yet every Thursday, four new rolls appeared outside our door, and since we knew we wouldn't use it all, we decided to get creative.

First, we made the Tower of TP: a nice pyramid against the bathroom wall. But this wasn't getting rid of it, so we moved into the all-purpose phase. We used it for everything, even pucks for hall hockey. Still, there was all this toilet paper. That is, until our men's basketball team beat Kentucky. That night we unloaded our entire inventory. Out our sixteenth-story window, roll after roll unfurled into the night, wrapping the trees and cars below. The next morning there was a knock at the door. On the floor were four new rolls.

I'm older now, and I'd like to think that I've matured and wouldn't be so wasteful this time around. But I know myself too well. Although I don't toss toilet paper from tall buildings anymore, I do find myself wasting something far more important: God's grace and forgiveness. Maybe we all do. We toss it out the window, take it for granted, relying on the knowledge that there's always more. God's grace is free, but it has never been cheap. Just think of what it cost: not you or me, but Christ.

**Lord, help me never to take your grace for granted. Amen.**

# Wood Splitting

*Make it your ambition to lead a quiet life, to mind your own business and to work with your hands.* —**1 Thessalonians 4:11**

—⚬—

The first cut is tricky. Guess wrong, and you bury the ax to the hilt and have to spend the next five minutes trying to pull it out. Guess right, and there's a solid *thwack* that goes right through the wood, splitting it, sometimes exploding it in two. It's more art than science—a combination of force and desire, of skill and guesswork. Yet once you find the rhythm, there is an ease to it. A quiet joy comes over you that makes you smile at the purity of it all. Even on a winter's day, when the ground crunches and the leaves tinkle like shards of glass, there it is—that joy.

Of course, you may not care a thing for splitting wood. This may sound like agony to you. But aren't there things you do, simple things, that bring you joy, things that take you outside yourself and lift your heart to God?

Far too many of us have the mistaken idea that God can be found only at church on Sundays. Every day is filled with opportunities to experience God's presence. He is close, right under our noses, in the middle of those simple things we enjoy. If we could see this, then perhaps God would not seem so distant but would be as real as an ax in hand and as close as the January chill.

**Lord, help me find you in the simple things I enjoy. Amen.**

# True Grit

—⟋⟋⟋—

Don't ask me why, but I've been on this grits kick lately. I suppose it's the cold weather here at the start of a new year. I wake up to a hard frost, and a bowl of corn flakes just won't cut it. I want something to warm me up, something that will stick to my ribs—like grits. So I boil some water, pour in a pack of instant grits, and I'm all set.

I only wish cleanup were as easy. See, I have this bad habit of leaving a little too much behind, and you know what that means. That's right, while I'm off at work, my grits are busy bonding with the bowls and spoons. And after a day or two, when the grits have almost cemented, there's nothing left to do but roll up my sleeves and get down to scrubbing.

This got me thinking. Elbows deep in hot, sudsy water, I had a revelation. Here in the season of New Year's resolutions, of wishful thinking and slim resolve, we could all use a little more grit, a little more staying power. Especially when it comes to our relationship with Christ. So often, after the initial enthusiasm fades, we lose interest and let things slide. We stop reading our Bible. We don't attend church or youth group as regularly. As believers, however, our devotion must be steadfast.

**Lord, give me the grit to stick to what I start. Amen.**

# Investing My Time

*"For what will it profit them to gain the whole world and forfeit their life?"* —**Mark 8:36 NRSV**

It's after midnight. The game is *Risk*. Four teenagers are gathered around a small table, plotting to take over the world. Two of them are standing; I can hear the dice clinking in their hands. *Mongolia attacking China.* "C'mon, sixes!" one says.

But like I said, it's late. And two hours from now, I know exactly what will happen. The young Caesars and Napoleons will grow tired, and world conquest will not seem so interesting. They'll be sitting instead of standing, ready to get it over with. One by one they will all drift away from the table until all that's left are a few scattered armies and the red-and-white dice.

A lot of things are like that. They seem important at first, but then something happens. The dice get cold, and we just lose interest. Now, I was taught that if you started something you should see it through to the end. The truth is, however, that some things aren't worth finishing. Indeed, there are times when we need to walk away from the table and invest our energy someplace else. We can't do everything. Our time is limited. So we must decide where our time is best spent.

**Lord, help me decide where best to invest my time. Amen.**

# Between a Rock and a Hard Place

*Though you have made me see troubles, many and bitter,
you will restore my life again.* —**Psalm 71:20**

—ɯ—

It's what climbers call a chimney, a crevice in the rock just large enough to squeeze yourself into. This one began halfway up a ledge and ran about forty feet straight up through the rock. Sensing an opportunity, I scrambled up the ledge, chalked up, and climbed in. The rock was slick and cold, and there was little I could do but brace my hands against one wall and my back against the other.

Climbing like this was a slow, painful process. My back hurt; my arms ached from bracing. I wanted to go back the way I had come. By this time, however, I was more than twenty feet off the ground. A fall would hurt more than my pride. I didn't see any way to shimmy down safely, and I was too tired to keep climbing. I was stuck.

Maybe you know the feeling: you don't like where you are, but you don't see any way out. Then again, all dark places aren't necessarily bad places. In fact, it's in some of these *spiritual chimneys* that God does his best work. For it's there in the dark, when you've exhausted all your resources, when you've tried everything but God, that God finally breaks through. It's there that a new you is born.

**Lord, use the circumstances of my life to remake me into the person you want me to be. Amen.**

# Nothing Is Impossible

*But Jesus looked at them and said, "For mortals it is impossible, but for God all things are possible." —Matthew 19:26 NRSV*

———

We were halfway through the game when the bottom fell out. Lightning flashed across the sky, illuminating dark-bellied clouds. We scurried off the field as the first big drops fell. Huddling in the dugout, we sat and watched the puddles connect like beads of mercury until the infield was one big lake.

When the rain finally stopped, our coach sloshed over to the canteen to talk to the umpires. I'd already packed up my cleats and glove when he returned. I figured they'd call it off. "We're gonna play," he said. We looked on in disbelief as the ground crew went to work on the field. They drained what they could before burning off the rest. I've never seen anything like it. Two hours and several hotdogs later, we were playing. "It just goes to show you," Mom said, "you can't ever tell."

The same is true about people. *He'll never change. She's a lost cause. It's just easier to write them off, to pack our bags and move on, than it is to worry over them, right?* Wrong. You see, our Lord loves the long shot. He loves making the impossible possible. He delights in fixing the field and getting us back into the game. So don't give up on your friends. And don't give up on yourself. God certainly hasn't.

**Lord, let me help you in making the impossible possible. Amen.**

# Castles in the Sand

*What do people gain from all the toil*
*at which they toil under the sun?* —**Ecclesiastes 1:3 NRSV**

—⚏—

A winter day. The tide is out; the beach is wide. I'm jogging halfway between the water and the dunes, where the sand is packed and it's easier to run. Above me, a few castles dot the sand, placed a safe distance from the surf. The tide is so far out, the waves so far away, that I'm tempted to believe these structures will survive the night.

But I know better. Tonight the waves will swell as the tide comes in. Wet, moon-streaked fingers will come clawing up the sand, filling the moats, tearing down the towers with their firecracker flags. A little boy's or little girl's efforts will be lost, swept out to sea.

Maybe the writer of Ecclesiastes was right: What do we have to show for all of our hard work? In the end, does it really matter if we won the state championship or put on a great chorus show or built the prize-winning float in the homecoming parade? In five years, will anyone remember? Will anyone even care? What if we could do something that would matter? The truth is, we can. What we do as Christians has eternal significance. Because it is given to God, it is never lost or swept away. It echoes into eternity. So take heart—your work is not in vain.

**Lord, let all that I do be done for you. Amen.**

# Pruning

*"He cuts off every branch in me that bears no fruit, while every branch that does bear fruit he prunes so that it will be even more fruitful." —John 15:2*

———∿∿∿———

A few years ago our men's group met early one morning to work on the hedges around the church. Bearing a vast assortment of hand clippers, rakes, and coffee mugs, they looked out from beneath their camouflage caps, finished their coffee, and waded in. Yet as the morning wore on and the coffee wore off, the men began to tire. Three hours later, they still hadn't made much progress.

I don't know whose idea the chainsaw was. At the time, however, it must have seemed like a stroke of brilliance. Soon the air was full of rumbling saws and whistling men. Blades whirred, branches fell. Sunday morning came, and everyone gathered outside to survey the damage. The men had had a night to sleep on it, and now they seemed a little less sure of themselves. One woman, however, was completely sure: she wasn't pleased. *They needed pruning, not destroying! There's nothing left but the stumps!*

Sometimes it feels like God's doing the same thing. Because God doesn't want anything to hinder our relationship with him, he often prunes such things from our lives. This kind of cutting is never pleasant, but it has its purpose. God isn't trying to hurt us. Rather, he wants to perfect us so that we can bear more fruit for him.

**Lord, cut away all that hinders my relationship with you. Amen.**

# Sacrificing

*I appeal to you therefore, brothers and sisters, by the mercies of God, to present your bodies as a living sacrifice.* —**Romans 12:1 NRSV**

—∿—

*The situation was grim. We were pinned down behind an overturned wheelbarrow and a rusty old Radio Flyer wagon. Pecans whistled through the air, plinking off our makeshift barricade. We were out of ammo. There was nothing to do but retreat. We made a beeline for the house, but they were waiting for us. Pecans rained down from the sky. I twirled in a slow-motion fall, convulsing on the ground.*

Back then we normally "died" at least twice a day during our battles. It was expected. We all wanted to play the hero; we all were willing to make "the supreme sacrifice." I confess that it was easier then, when it was just make-believe. I'm a Marine now; the bullets we use are real. We live with the knowledge that we could die in battle and that we must be willing to make "the supreme sacrifice."

But that's not the kind of sacrifice Paul is talking about in his letter to the Romans. You see, God doesn't usually ask us to sacrifice our lives—at least, not all at once. Instead, God calls us to be living sacrifices, to make small sacrifices every day, to die to self, and to live for him. While this kind of sacrifice may never make the six o'clock news, know that it's this kind of daily commitment that is the true measure of the Christian life.

**Lord, help me daily to do those little things that matter to you. Amen.**

# Things Fall Apart

*So is my word that goes out from my mouth:*
  *It will not return to me empty,*
*but will accomplish what I desire.* —Isaiah 55:11

—⁓—

Grandpa Johnny was not one for disorder. You know the type: a place for everything, and everything in its place. That was him. Well, every autumn, when the leaves let go and piled ankle deep on his lawn, I'd come over, rake in hand, ready to do battle. But you know how that goes. By the time you finish the backyard, the freshly raked front is already filling with late arrivals. You just can't win.

It's that way with our spiritual lives. We strive for order; we want everything in its place, yet more often than not our best efforts fail. We just can't seem to get it right. With so much to do, we end up feeling frustrated and overwhelmed. It makes you want to scream. Or quit.

The truth is that we can't do it by ourselves. We will never get it all together—not without God. Think about it. From the very beginning, God is the one who brought order to chaos, who formed the worlds, and gave life through his Word. Sure, we can choose to keep struggling. We can choose to trust in our own strength. Or we can trust in him and his Word.

**Lord, bring order to my life. Amen.**

# Just Enough

*And I pray that you ... may be filled to the measure of all the fullness of God.* **—Ephesians 3:17, 19**

—m—

I'm not sure how long I'd been driving on empty. The needle had bottomed out, and as I scanned the interstate ahead for an exit, I wasn't sure I'd make it home. After a few miles, however, I spotted a gas station and quickly pulled in. Only then did I realize that I'd left my ATM card at home. A quiet panic came over me as I searched my Jeep for cash. Luckily, I found two dollars in the glove compartment and some change under the seat. It was just enough.

This is fine for my Jeep. After all, I hardly ever fill it up; I get just enough to get me where I want to go. But what about our spirits? How often are we cruising around on less than a quarter of a tank? And when we come to church, do we want just enough Jesus to get us through the week? just enough to make us feel good about ourselves? just enough to save us but not transform us?

The apostle Paul tells us that God doesn't want us to walk around feeling empty. Instead, God wants us to come to him and be filled with love, to be so full of his love that, like a glass filled to the brim, it sloshes out on everyone we meet.

**Lord, fill me with love for you. Amen.**

# No Trespassing

*O LORD, you have searched me
and you know me.* —**Psalm 139:1**

—∿—

I noticed a building under renovation one day when I was walking through downtown Albuquerque. It was almost noon. The sun was blazing down from the biggest sky I'd ever seen, so bright and hot that even the buildings seemed to crouch together. Except this one. It was an older building, standing alone, surrounded by a fence topped with barbed wire. Black signs screaming *NO TRESPASSING* dotted the fence, and yet, even from the sidewalk I could see that the building had been gutted. It was nothing but a shell. How strange. All this fence and wire protecting what? Just emptiness.

Then again, maybe it isn't strange at all. We put on a good face, hide behind fake smiles, do whatever it takes to keep others out and protect ourselves. We are afraid that if someone gets too close, they might see how empty we are inside. But God sees through all this, and, miracle of miracles, he loves us anyway. If only we could let that seep into our bones. Then we might let love come in; then we might embrace God just as he embraces us.

**Lord, thank you for your unconditional, unchanging love. Amen.**

# Traffic

*"The LORD gave and the LORD has taken away;
may the name of the LORD be praised."* —**Job 1:21**

—⁂—

Ahead, I watch the brake lights wink on one by one. The traffic slows to a crawl and then stops. I poke my head out the window to see what's going on. Cars are stretched out for miles, and not one is moving. Fifteen minutes later, I've turned off the Jeep. I'm sitting on the hood, restless and angry. A few other people have crawled from their cars; they're standing with the doors open, looking for any sign of movement. Yet here we are, completely stuck, going nowhere.

I would like to say that I remained calm and was able to take it in stride. But I didn't, not that day. When we got moving, I was still ticked. I drove with clenched fists, scanning the side of the road, looking for some clue—an overturned truck, a flaming car, anything. Even now I don't know the reason.

I guess I can just file it with all the other things I don't understand. For example, why is there so much suffering and injustice in the world? Why do some children develop cancer? Why can't all Christians get along? Although I may never know the answers in this life, I trust that we all somehow fit into God's plan. Things may not make sense to us, but they do make sense to God. There will be daily aggravations. Some days will even bring disaster. Even so, we must trust him.

**Lord, help me trust you when life doesn't make sense. Amen.**

# A Reminder

*Give thanks to the LORD, call on his name;*
*make known among the nations what he has done.*
—1 Chronicles 16:8

—⚬⚬⚬—

On the wall there are black-and-white pictures of broken houses. A closer look confirms that they are in ruins, left to the elements, left to weather and rot. The pictures are captivating, exquisite in their own way. And from the outside looking in, I marvel at the beauty of it all.

Yet I wonder about the people who lived in these broken houses. I say *houses* because I dare not call them homes. That seems far too personal, far too damaging to my mood. After all, I've been in houses like these. I worked on them and in them; I met those who lived there, who did not see the art. And I walked away and, for the most part, forgot them.

But every once in a while, I see a picture and remember: the poverty, hopelessness, and quiet desperation carved in their faces. It makes me want to scream at the injustice of it all and at my own calloused heart. Yet, it also makes me profoundly thankful. All that I have, all that you have, are gifts from our gracious God. May our lives be our gift to him.

**Lord, thank you for all the many ways you've blessed me. Amen.**

# Carpe Diem

*Be very careful, then, how you live—not as unwise but as wise, making the most of every opportunity.* —**Ephesians 5:15-16**

—⟋⟍—

I've never cared much for graduation speeches. It's not that I haven't heard a few good ones, but most of them seem to indicate that if you play your cards right, you'll be living the good life a few years down the road. I don't believe that's the right message. What they *should* say is, "Carpe diem!" "Seize the day." Live now.

Now, I realize there are risks with this kind of approach. Some of these speech givers may be afraid that if they encourage you to live now, you might party too much, flunk out of school, and end up somewhere south of skid row. Yet what they're telling you now isn't any better: that life begins after high school, or when you get your first big job, or when you find and marry the perfect man or woman.

The trouble with this view of life is that life never really begins. It's always "out there," waiting somewhere beyond the horizon. And so we muddle through the present, waiting for everything to be just right before we can start living. Yet that's not what the Bible teaches at all. Rather, it reminds us over and over that every day, every moment, is an opportunity. It's up to us to make the most of it.

**Lord, help me make the most of each day you give me. Amen.**

# One Wheelbarrow at a Time

*Teach us to number our days aright,*
*that we may gain a heart of wisdom.* —**Psalm 90:12**

—⟋⟍—

It wasn't far from the woodpile to our porch, but for a scrawny kid like me, it felt like miles. Nevertheless, every afternoon when I got home from school, it was my job to gather in enough wood for the night. So I would load up the wheelbarrow with fat pieces of oak, trying to get enough in one trip.

One day my dad came home early and found me struggling with the task. Even though I had dropped a few pieces along the way, I was still having trouble. I'd lift with a grunt, teeter on for a few steps, and then stop to catch my breath. "That's a lot of wood you've got there," he said. "Maybe you should take a smaller load."

Maybe *you* should, too. One of the dangers of being young is that we try to do too much. We're afraid of missing out, and so we have a hard time saying no to anything. Even worse, sometimes we try to do *everything* all at once. Basketball. Debate team. Youth group president. "Sure. I can do that." Well, you can, but at what cost? In my experience, my relationship with God usually suffers most. The truth is, when you're too busy for God, you're just too busy.

**Lord, forgive me when I've been too busy for you. Amen.**

# Pointless

*So that you may become blameless and pure, children of God without fault in a crooked and depraved generation, in which you shine like stars in the universe as you hold out the word of life.* **—Philippians 2:15-16**

———

My dog, Jake, is a pointer, but he's not a very good one. Not because he doesn't point—he straightens his tail, flattens his head, and lifts his paw just like he should—but because he's not very picky. Be it bird, discarded bottle, or soda can, it really does not matter. He'll point at anything.

Pointing comes naturally for him. It's in his blood. Even so, he has to be taught what to point at. That's where I come in. I've never been much of a hunter, so I don't much care about him pointing out certain types of game. But it would be nice if he were more consistent, if I knew that whatever he pointed to was something good. Then again, wouldn't it be nice if we all were a little more consistent?

As Christians, we are called to point others to what is pure, good, and noble. We are called to be imitators of God, to shine like stars, guiding others to Christ. Often, however, instead of showing others how God desires us to live, we allow the world to instruct our living and form our habits. When this happens, our pointing becomes *pointless,* and our witness is watered down.

**Lord, help me always to point others to you. Amen.**

# Lost and Found

*Then Jesus told them this parable: "Suppose one of you has a hundred sheep and loses one of them. Does he not leave the ninety-nine in the open country and go after the lost sheep until he finds it?"* —**Luke 15:3-4**

———∾∾———

I didn't see him wander off. I'd gotten so used to Jake running back and forth that I didn't notice when he slipped off to investigate a side trail. But just like that, he was gone. So I dropped my pack, sat down, and waited. Still no Jake. I got up again and called him. Up and down the trail I went, calling his name.

I didn't know what to do. It was such a large area—hundreds of acres of wilderness, so many places he could be. It was like searching for a needle in a haystack, so I gave up. All the way home I stewed. *He should have known better. He shouldn't have wandered off.*

Two nights later, I drove back to Asheville to get him. Someone had found him and called the number on his collar. As I drove, I couldn't help feeling guilty. How quickly I'd grown tired of looking for him. He had wandered away, and I had given up the search. I'm so thankful that Jesus is different. Jesus never stops looking for us, and he always knows just where to find us. And though he doesn't condone our wandering or prevent us from getting hurt in the process, he's always ready to bring us back into the fold.

**Lord, thank you for seeking us when we wander. Amen.**

# The Question

*"She will give birth to a son, and you are to give him the name Jesus, because he will save his people from their sins."* —**Matthew 1:21**

—∿—

How odd it seemed to be planting a cross at night, especially in December. But that's what we did. There in the churchyard, in the faint glowing headlights, with Christmas music coming through the rolled-down windows of a truck, we dug a hole and planted it.

Digging a hole in the dark is like digging your grave, and though my friends and I talked our way through it, I was glad when we were done, when our cross was up and standing. The cement was still wet around the bottom, but there wasn't much left to do, so we shook hands and parted ways. Still, I couldn't help lingering. It was warm out, more spring than winter, and my thoughts turned to Easter and to another cross.

Sweet baby Jesus grew up and was nailed to a cross. I doubt that anyone who saw him in the manger guessed he would end up there, giving his life for our salvation. What about you? What kind of person will you grow up to be? What effect will your life have on countless others?

**Lord, help me make a difference in the lives of others. Amen.**

# Enthusiastic Living

*Whatever you do, work at it with all your heart, as working for the Lord, not for men.* —**Colossians 3:23**

—⚭—

It was almost dark when I noticed them: a group of boys playing soccer on a vacant lot. In the fluorescent glare of a single light, I could see that their clothes were dirty from a long day in the fields. Patched with duct tape, their soccer ball was more silver than white. As it rolled it caught the light, reflecting like a mirror ball. For goals, overturned buckets and tree stumps sufficed.

Now, I don't know much Spanish. And I know even less about soccer. But there was a music in their shouts and laughter that needed no translation. It was the simple sound of joy, of enthusiasm. And though there were no crowds to impress, they were playing like their lives depended on it.

Maybe your closet isn't filled with the kind of clothes you'd like. Instead of a new car, maybe you drive an old clunker. So what? In life, having a good attitude matters a lot more than having the right equipment. And as believers, we should have the best attitude of all. We certainly have a lot to be enthusiastic about.

**Lord, give me new eyes to see and celebrate my blessings. Amen.**

# Bargain Shopping

*Remember your Creator*
  *in the days of your youth,*
*before the days of trouble come*
  *and the years approach when you will say,*
  *"I find no pleasure in them."* —**Ecclesiastes 12:1**

—⟋⟍—

This is one of the busiest shopping days of the year. On December 26, the stores open early, ready to greet the swarm of shoppers looking for a good deal. In fact, many of these shoppers have waited until now, and with good reason. Prices are slashed. Stores are making room for new inventory. There are great bargains to be had simply by waiting until after Christmas.

The trouble is we can have this same mind-set when it comes to our faith, thinking that the price of being a Christian is just too high while we're young. We may feel that there is a lot we would miss out on by trying to be a disciple right now, that it would be easier and less of a sacrifice if we put off following Christ until we are out of school, out of college, and ready to settle down.

The truth is, however, that Christian living never goes on sale. The cost is always high. But, the sooner we accept the cross of Christ, the sooner we enter into the richness and joyfulness of life that he offers and, perhaps, the fewer bad choices we'll make along the way.

**Lord, help me take up your cross while I am still young. Amen.**

# Changing Gears

*Because of the LORD's great love we are not consumed,*
*for his compassions never fail.* —**Lamentations 3:22**

—ɷ—

I'm not sure how Dad survived teaching me to drive his old Toyota. It had a manual transmission with three small pedals in the floor for my two oversized feet. Being the uncoordinated person that I am, it didn't work out too well. We would leave the driveway in a series of fits, as I constantly confused the brake and the clutch. I can still picture Dad holding on for dear life, braced against the dash, while I was changing gears. We hiccuped along like this for weeks. I'm sure Dad wondered if I'd ever get the hang of it.

It can sometimes seem that way with the Christian life as well. For new believers—and even not-so-new believers—there can be a certain amount of awkwardness mixed in with our excitement. It's easy to become frustrated and discouraged as we find ourselves making the same old mistakes or falling back into old habits. But don't give up on yourself. God understands that you are trying and that you are eager to learn. He is patient and ready to help you.

**Lord, thank you for being patient when my progress is slow. Amen.**

# Chasing

*Draw near to God, and he will draw near to you.* —**James 4:8 NRSV**

—⟶⟶⟶—

I don't know why I love the chase. I think it's written in my genes. Throw something out there—a football, a Frisbee, whatever—and I'll run after it. I can't help myself. To see it sailing through the air makes me want it. It's that simple. Maybe that's why I would always ask Dad to hit me deep fly balls.

Some days he would hit them just right; other days they would rocket over my head. On those days, it seemed that no matter how hard I tried, I could never catch up. Soon I'd grow tired of all the chasing and running and never catching.

I am thankful, however, that it's not this way with God. This is not some endless chase. God longs for us to seek him, and when we do, he doesn't run from us but comes to us, drawing us even closer. God is not like those line drives that go whizzing overhead. Instead, he meets us right where we are.

**Lord, thank you for meeting me where I am. Amen.**

# Misplaced

*Even though I walk*
*   through the valley of the shadow of death,*
*I will fear no evil,*
*   for you are with me.* **—Psalm 23:4**

———

I have this bad habit of misplacing things. What's worse, how-ever, is my tendency to misplace *myself*. Not that I'm lost. Rather, it's that I'm not sure if where I *am* is on the way to where I want to *go*. Usually this is just the result of a wrong turn or a missed exit—nothing major. For a minute I'm disoriented, but as soon as I see a sign or recognize a landmark, the feeling fades.

It's not so easy when you're in the woods, though. There, the trails often aren't well marked, and after wandering around for a while, everything starts to look the same. It's easy to get turned around. I search for a sign that I'm on the right path, and now my steps aren't as confident. I try to retrace my steps but find that I can't. I've gotten *misplaced*.

Occasionally, we suffer a similar kind of spiritual disorientation. What we thought was God's plan now appears to be a dead end, and with it comes an awful uncertainty. We wonder where we went wrong; we start to panic. Yet maybe in our search for a sure sign we've overlooked the obvious. Could it be that God has led us into unfamiliar territory not to terrify us but to teach us?

**Lord, help me trust in you when my path is unclear. Amen.**

# Putting It Together

*"In the same way, let your light shine before others, so that they may see your good works and give glory to your Father in heaven."*
—**Matthew 5:16 NRSV**

———

On the box, in big bold letters, were the words *Some assembly required*. I should have considered this a warning. But because the box was small and I had the tools required, I didn't think it would be hard. After all, this was just your basic, run-of-the-mill lawn mower.

Hindsight being what it is, I should have handed over the extra ten bucks for the one already assembled. Soon I found myself surrounded by levers, axles, and bolts. Even the instruction manual wasn't much help. There were too many instructions and not enough pictures. See, I'm a visual learner, and that afternoon I needed detailed pictures to show what went where. I needed to see it all put together.

That's what the world needs as well. When your friends are going through tough times and are looking for answers, they may not want you quoting scripture. Rather, they want to see it all put together. They look to you, expecting you to live what you believe. And while this doesn't mean that God's Word is unimportant, it may just make a lot more sense to them when they can see how it works in real life.

**Lord, help me model the truths I believe. Amen.**

# A Long Rain

*See! The winter is past;*
  *the rains are over and gone.*
*Flowers appear on the earth;*
  *the season of singing has come.* —Song of Songs 2:11-12

—⚏—

I broke camp early, at first light. Already the wind was whipping through the passes, clapping the limbs of oak and sycamore together like awkward hands. I slung my pack over my shoulders and started down the trail as the first big drops began to fall.

Two hours later, the rain was still coming down and the trail had turned to soup. I tried to pick my way through it, stepping carefully from stone to stone, hoping to keep my feet dry. I didn't want a boot full of water or the blisters that come with it. The trouble is, there just weren't enough stones. And since I didn't have waterproof boots, I just slogged through it the best I could. I was wet, miserable, and cold.

Looking up at those gunmetal clouds, it was hard to imagine that the rain would ever stop, that somewhere on the other side of all the misery the sun was shining. And yet that's what believers are called to do. We must trust in God's goodness even when life isn't what we hoped.

**Lord, help me trust in you when life is bleak and gray. Amen.**

# When the Bottom Drops Out

*"For I know the plans I have for you," declares the LORD, "plans to prosper you and not to harm you, plans to give you hope and a future." —Jeremiah 29:11*

—m—

A popular ride at a local amusement park is the Drop Zone. It's not a roller coaster, but a two-hundred-foot tower with seats attached to the sides. They strap you in at the bottom, and you slowly clink your way to the top. Then you fall. The air is sucked from your lungs, and it feels like your stomach has found a new home between your ears. The brakes hiss, and your body seems to fold in two. You stagger away only to get back in line, ready to do it again. It's like we enjoy this feeling of falling.

Or do we? When someone you love dies unexpectedly, when your mother or father loses a job, when you find out your parents are getting a divorce, then what? Once again, there's the sensation of falling. Your stomach drops, only it's not fun this time. Where is God at times like these? And if he really loves you, why does he let these things happen?

I don't have the answer. The fact is that bad things happen. Even so, God has promised us that he is looking out for us, that our future is secure with him—even when the bottom drops out.

**Lord, when something bad happens, help me remember that you are with me. Amen.**

# Fixing

*On hearing this, Jesus said, "It is not the healthy who need a doctor, but the sick." —Matthew 9:12*

—∿—

I'm a "fixer" by nature. I guess most guys are. When confronted by a problem—whether personal, mechanical, or spiritual—I want to fix it. Maybe that's why I like home repair. I know how to fix a leaking roof or a sagging floor. Provided the time, tools, and materials, I can take care of it. In a few days, the roof will be watertight; the floor will be sound. Problem solved.

The trouble is that most things in life aren't like that. Most problems don't get ironed out in a week. A friend is injured in a car wreck, a family member is diagnosed with cancer, and I want to fix it, to make it all better. But a hammer and nails won't work here. There's no board to cut or room to paint, and I feel ill-equipped to respond.

Yet I've learned that it's not about the tools I carry or even my abilities. There is another who fixes: the Great Physician, who was also a carpenter. He knew the limitations of wood and nails. He also knew the needs of his people. So the next time you feel overwhelmed, when you don't know how to ease the loss or make the hurt disappear, refer them to another, to Jesus. Ask him to be their healer and comforter.

**Lord, comfort my friends and family who are hurting. Amen.**

# Fear Not

*So do not fear, for I am with you;*
  *do not be dismayed, for I am your God.*
*I will strengthen you and help you.* —Isaiah 41:10

———

My dog, Jake, is afraid of thunderstorms. From what I've learned, this is true for many dogs. Most dogs don't like loud noises, particularly thunder. So I suppose Jake is normal. What isn't normal, however, is the way he reacts. The first time I left him home alone during a storm, he shredded the back door and broke a window. When I came home, I found him huddled in the shower, bleeding and terrified.

I can sympathize. We all have our fears, whether it's the fear of heights or snakes or failure or speaking in public. That doesn't mean we should allow ourselves to be controlled by them. You see, there's a difference between a healthy caution and the kind of fear that paralyzes. It's OK to be extra cautious crossing a rope bridge over a river. That makes sense. What's not OK is the fear that keeps us from trying out for the team, the fear of rejection that won't let us speak to that special person we like, the fear that prevents us from sharing our faith.

As Christians, we believe there is nothing in this life—no problem, fear, or difficulty—that God can't help us overcome. He is our help and our shield. And he will give us the courage to face our fears.

**Lord, help me face my fears. Amen.**

# Overexposed

*The mind of sinful man is death, but the mind controlled by the Spirit is life and peace; the sinful mind is hostile to God.* —**Romans 8:6-7**

—⁓—

It's a long walk from the parking lot to the barracks, especially in four inches of snow. Then again, I hardly notice the cold. I've been training in it for weeks now. I guess I've gotten used to it. It makes me wonder if the constant exposure has made me less sensitive. Thirty degrees just doesn't seem that cold anymore.

I think it has more to do with my mind than with my body. Physically, I haven't changed at all. I have the same body here that I had in South Carolina. Mentally, however, I've become accustomed to colder temperatures. When there's snow on the ground, I go running in shorts.

This ability to adapt, however, isn't always a good thing. In many instances, what once shocked and horrified us, now no longer fazes us. Think about the shows we watch, the music we listen to. Much of it would have been considered obscene just ten years ago. But gradually we have gotten used to it. Now it almost feels normal. Yet maybe all this exposure has only made our conscience less sensitive.

**Lord, are the shows I watch and the music I listen to pleasing to you? Amen.**

# Departing Now

*Brothers, we do not want you to be ignorant about those who fall asleep, or to grieve like the rest of men, who have no hope.* —1 Thessalonians 4:13

—⁓—

The terminal was almost empty. The passengers had boarded the plane. The good-byes had been said; there was nothing left to do but leave. Yet I could not pull myself away from the window. I couldn't help lingering. It seemed too soon, too final, this departure. So I stood there with my coffee, with a newspaper folded under my arm. I could feel the cold coming through the glass, and I shivered at the separation.

I had a similar feeling at my grandmother's funeral. She died so unexpectedly; none of us was ready. So there I stood, staring at a closed casket and a freshly dug grave, struck by the suddenness of it all. She had already departed, and I hadn't said good-bye. Again, I shivered at the separation.

Yet I know that I will see her again. The separation that now seems so great will disappear in the blink of an eye. Yes, a time will come when there will be no more good-byes, no more sad departures. That is why we don't have to fear death as Christians. It has no power over us; it is not final. For believers, death is just a doorway.

**Lord, thank you for making a way for me to spend all eternity with you. Amen.**

# Rifle Inspection

*"For the LORD does not see as mortals see; they look on the outward appearance, but the LORD looks on the heart."* —1 Samuel 16:7 NRSV

The M16A2 service rifle weighs 8.79 pounds and is approximately 40 inches long. Because of its size, you wouldn't think it would take long to clean. But I can't tell you how many hours I spent cleaning it while I was at Officer Training School. The outside was relatively easy. A few minutes with a toothbrush would do the trick. The inside, however, required more work.

Because it took more time and effort, there were times when I didn't give it the attention it needed. It was just easier to worry about the outside. Even so, my sergeant instructors never failed to check. They weren't impressed by a shiny exterior. The inside must be clean or the rifle will fail to work properly. And if the rifle fails, so will the Marine.

The same is true for us as Christians. When our lives are clogged with sin, we can't function the way God has designed us. No matter how clean we may appear to everyone around us, if we are messy on the inside, we won't be able to make the right decisions when it counts.

**Lord, cleanse me of secret sins. Amen.**

# Homework

*You are not your own; you were bought at a price.* —1 Corinthians 6:19-20

—⁂—

I've never cared for homework. Whenever we had time in class, I tried to get all of my homework done, so that when I got home I didn't have to think about it. The last thing I wanted to do after school was more school.

The same is true now that I'm a Marine. The trouble is that I don't stop being a Marine when I'm on liberty or even when I have a few weeks off. All the standards still apply, whether I'm in uniform or not. I'm a Marine twenty-four hours a day, seven days a week, whether I feel like it or not.

Come to think of it, that's how it is for Christians. We don't stop being Christians when we leave church or when we're on spring break. It's not a nine-to-five job. There's always homework; this responsibility goes with us wherever we go. As believers, we never take a day off from being Christian.

**Lord, help me behave as a Christian wherever I go. Amen.**